I DECLARE

ALSO BY JOEL OSTEEN

Every Day a Friday
Every Day a Friday Journal
Daily Readings from Every Day a Friday
Your Best Life Now
Daily Readings from Your Best Life Now
Starting Your Best Life Now
Your Best Life Now Study Guide
Your Best Life Now for Moms
Your Best Life Begins Each Morning
Your Best Life Now Journal

Available from FaithWords
wherever books are sold.

I DECLARE

31 PROMISES TO SPEAK OVER YOUR LIFE

JOEL OSTEEN

New York Boston Nashville

FaithWords

Hachette Book Group

237 Park Avenue

New York, NY 10017

www.faithwords.com

Printed in the United States of America

RRD-C

First Edition: September 2012

10 9 8 7 6 5 4 3 2 1

FaithWords is a division of Hachette Book Group, Inc.

The FaithWords name and logo are trademarks of Hachette Book Group, Inc.

The Hachette Speakers Bureau provides a wide range of authors for speaking events. To find out more, go to www.hachettespeakersbureau.com or call (866) 376-6591.

The publisher is not responsible for websites (or their content) that are not owned by the publisher.

Library of Congress Control Number: 2012942697

INTRODUCTION

Our words have creative power. Whenever we speak something, either good or bad, we give life to what we are saying. Too many people say negative things about themselves, about their families, and about their futures. They say things such as, "I'll never be successful. This sickness will get the best of me. Business is so slow I don't think I will make it. Flu season is coming. I'll probably catch it."

They don't realize they are prophesying their futures. The Scripture says, "We will eat the fruit of our words." That means we will get exactly what we've been saying.

Here is the key; you've got to send your words out in the direction you want your life to go. You cannot talk defeat and expect to have victory. You can't talk lack and expect to have abundance. You will produce what you say. If you want to know what you will be like five years from now, just listen to what you are saying about yourself. With our words we can either bless our futures or we can curse our futures. That's why we should never say, "I'm not a good parent. I'm unattractive. I'm clumsy. I can't do anything right. I'll probably get laid off."

No, those thoughts may come to your mind, but don't make the mistake of verbalizing them. The moment you speak them out, you allow them to take root. There have been plenty of times where I've thought something negative and I'm just about to say it, but I'll catch myself and think, *No. I'll zip it up. I'm not speaking defeat into my future. I'm not speaking failure over my life. I will turn it around and speak favor into my future. I will declare, "I'm blessed. I'm strong. I'm healthy. This will be a great year."* When you do that, you are blessing your future.

I have written this book of thirty-one declarations so you can bless your future one day at a time, one month at a time. My hope is that you will take just a moment each day to bless your future with one of these positive, inspiring, and encouraging declarations. If you read one declaration and story each day, I believe you will put yourself in a position for God's blessings.

When we were looking to renovate the former Compaq Center in Houston so it could serve as the new Lakewood Church, our architects told us the project would cost millions more than we'd originally estimated. I was shocked by the figures they gave us. After I got up off the ground, I thought, *That's impossible. I could never raise that much money. There is no way that will happen.*

The thoughts were there, but I knew better than to verbalize them. My attitude was, *If I prophesy my future I want to prophesy something good. I'm not saying what I feel. I'm not saying what it looks like in the real world. No, I'm saying what God says about me.*

My declaration was, "God is supplying all of our needs. He is Jehovah-Jireh; the Lord our Provider. This may seem impossible but I know God can do the impossible. Where God gives vision He always provides provision."

I made sure to have a report of victory and we saw this dream come to pass. Proverbs 18:21 says, "Life and death are in the power of our tongue." What are you saying about your future? What are you saying about your family? What are you saying about your finances? Make sure the words you are sending out are in the direction you want your life to go.

If you're a baseball fan, you probably know who José Lima was. During the 1990s he was the star pitcher for the Houston Astros. One season he won twenty-one games and was considered one of the best pitchers in the league. But something interesting happened. When the Astros moved from the Astrodome to their new ballpark downtown, the fence in left field was much closer than the fence in the Astrodome. And of course, this favors the hitters. It makes it more difficult on the pitchers.

The first time José Lima went to the new ballpark he stood on the mound. When he looked out into left field and saw how close the fence was, the first words out of his mouth were, "I'll never be able to pitch in here. The fence is way too close."

Do you know he went from being a twenty-one-game winner to being a sixteen-game loser? It was one of the biggest negative turnarounds in Astros history. What happened? He prophesied his future. Those negative thoughts came, and instead of ignoring them, he made the mistake of speaking them out. When you speak it out you're giving life to your faith. As Proverbs 6:2 says, "We are snared by the words of our mouth."

When I was a boy there was a gentleman who owned the company that took care of our church grounds. He was a very nice man, kind and friendly. But he always had a negative report. Every time I talked to him he told me how hard life was and how business was slow and his equipment was breaking down. He was having problems at home. One of his children was acting up, on and on. I saw him twice a week for probably ten years. I cannot remember one time when he did not have a negative report. And I'm not making light of his situation. The point is he was prophesying defeat. He was cursing his future. He didn't realize he was being snared by the words of his mouth.

Sadly, when he was about fifty-five years old, he became very sick. He spent the next two or three years in and out of hospitals. He ended up dying a very sad and lonely death. I couldn't help but think that he had been predicting this sad end his entire life because he was always talking about how he would never make it to his retirement years. He got what he was calling in.

You may be in a difficult time right now, but let me challenge you. Don't use your words to describe the situation. Use your words to change the situation. Use this book as your guide for declaring your victory each day. Declare health. Declare favor. Declare abundance.

You give life to your faith by what you say. All through the day we should go around saying, "I have the favor of God. I can do all things through Christ. I am blessed. I'm strong. I'm healthy." When you do that you just blessed your life. You just spoke favor into your future. If you get up in the morning feeling the blahs don't ever say, "This will be a lousy day. I don't want to go to work. I'm tired of dealing with these children." No, get up and say, "This is going to be a great day. I'm excited about my future. Something good is about to happen to me."

You should send your words out in the direction you want your life to go. Maybe you've been through a disappointment. A relationship didn't work out. You didn't get the promotion you were hoping for. But instead of complaining by saying, "Well, I should have known it. I never get any good breaks. Just my luck." No, your declaration should be, "I know when one door closes God will open up another door. What was meant for my harm God will use to my advantage. I'm not only coming out, I will come out better off than I was before."

Have a report of victory.

Here's what I've learned. You believe what you say about yourself more than what anybody else says. That's why on a regular basis we should say, "I'm blessed. I'm healthy. I'm strong. I'm valuable. I'm talented. I have a bright future." Those words go out of your mouth and come right back into your own ears. Over time they will create the same image on the inside.

I read about a doctor in Europe who had some very sick patients. They had been treated by traditional means but their health had not improved. So he gave them a very unusual prescription. He had them say three or four times an hour, "I am getting better and better, every day, in every way."

Over the next few months he had remarkable results. Many of those patients had not improved with traditional medications, but all of the sudden, they began to feel better and better.

What happened? As they heard themselves saying over and over, "I'm getting better. I'm improving. My health is coming back," those words began to create a new image on the inside. Before long, they started seeing themselves strong, healthy, and whole. Once you get a picture of it on the inside then God can bring it to pass on the outside. You could see your life go to a whole new level if you just zip up the negative words and start speaking faith and victory into your future.

I know people who are always tired and run-down. They are constantly saying, "I'm so tired. I just don't have any energy."

They've talked about it so long, it's become a reality. Do you know the more we talk about something, the more we draw it in? It's as if you are feeding it. If you get up in the morning and just talk about how you feel, how you're tired and how you won't make it, you are defeating yourself. You're digging your own hole.

Don't talk about the problem. Talk about the solution. The Scripture says, "Let the weak say, 'I am strong.'" Notice it doesn't say, "Let the weak talk about their weakness. Let the weak call five friends and discuss their weakness." "Let the weak complain about their weakness." No, it says in effect, "Let the weak say exactly the opposite of how they feel."

In other words, don't talk about the way you are. Talk about the way you want to be. If you get up in the morning feeling tired and lethargic, instead of complaining more than ever, you need to declare, "I am strong in the Lord. I am full of energy. My strength is being renewed. This will be a great day."

When you do that it will not only change how you feel, it also will change your attitude. You won't go out with a weak, defeated, victim mentality. You will go out with a victor mentality, with a spring in your step, with a smile on your face, with your shoulders back. Those words can literally help lift your spirit and cause you to see yourself and your circumstances in a whole new light.

You are one of a kind. You are a masterpiece. You are a prized possession. When you wake up in the morning and look in the mirror instead of getting depressed, instead of saying, "Oh, man. Look how old I look. Look at this gray hair. Look at these wrinkles," you need to smile and say, "Good morning, you beautiful thing. Good morning, you handsome thing. Good morning, you blessed, prosperous, successful, strong, talented, creative, confident, secure, disciplined, focused, highly favored child of the Most High God." Get it on the inside. Speak faith over your future!

I DECLARE

DAY ONE

I DECLARE God's incredible blessings over my life. I will see an explosion of God's goodness, a sudden widespread increase. I will experience the surpassing greatness of God's favor. It will elevate me to a level higher than I ever dreamed of. Explosive blessings are coming my way. This is my declaration.

A friend of mine wanted to attend a major university, but he needed a scholarship to pay for his tuition. He applied many months before the school year started. Even though his grades were good enough to get into the school, he was informed that there were no more scholarships available. So, he enrolled in a junior college instead.

It looked like his dream of going to the major university was over. It looked like the situation was permanent. All the facts said it would not to happen. But just a few weeks before school was to start, the scholarship office called back and said something had opened up. Instead of offering him the two-year partial scholarship he had applied for, they offered him a four-year total scholarship; an explosive blessing.

You may think your situation is permanent. You've been in it a long time. You don't see how you could ever rise any higher. All the facts are telling you it's impossible. But God is saying today, "You need to get ready. Where you are is not permanent. I have explosive blessings coming your way. I will increase you beyond your salary. I will bless you beyond your normal income. I will suddenly change things in your life."

That's how the word *explosion* is defined. It means, "sudden, widespread increase." That's what God wants to do for each one of us. Suddenly. You won't expect it. It's out of the ordinary and it's not small. It's not mediocre. It's widespread increase. That means it's so amazing you know it had to be the hand of God.

That's what happened to one gentleman. He stopped by the church a while back and brought a very large donation to the ministry. It was his tithe. He said he had received an inheritance from a family member he had never met before. In fact, he didn't even really know that they were related, but this man left him a gift that thrust his family to a whole new level. He was able to not only pay his house off but he also had paid off several other people's houses as well.

I don't know about you, but I'm believing for some long-lost relatives like that. I'm believing for explosive blessings.

I'm believing for explosive blessings.

The Apostle Paul talked about this in Ephesians 2:7 (AMP). He said that we would see "the unlimited, immeasurable, surpassing greatness of God's favor." He was saying we would see favor like we've never seen it before.

In the real world, it may look like you could never accomplish your dreams. You've already calculated how you'll never get out of debt. You've run all the numbers—but God is saying, "You haven't seen My explosive blessings. You haven't seen the surpassing greatness of My favor. I have blessings that will catapult you years ahead. I have increase that goes beyond your normal calculations."

I've learned God doesn't always take us in normal increments. There are times He will increase us little by little. We have to be faithful day in and day out. But when you come to one of these *explosive* blessings, instead of going from 7 to 8 to 9, God will take you from 7 to 8 to 63 to 64. That's widespread increase!

DAY TWO

....

I DECLARE I will experience
God's faithfulness. I will not worry.
I will not doubt. I will keep my trust
in Him, knowing that He will not
fail me. I will give birth to every
promise God put in my heart and I
will become everything God created
me to be. This is my declaration.

....

Every one of us has dreams and goals in our heart. There are promises that we are standing on. Maybe you are believing for a child to turn around, or believing to get healthy again, believing to start a business or to be in ministry. Deep down you know God has spoken that to your spirit. He has birthed it on the inside. But so often, because it's taking a long time and we've been through disappointments, we get negative and start thinking that it will not happen.

The reason many people don't see God's promises come to pass is because they become discouraged and give up too soon. But just because you don't see anything happening doesn't mean God is not working. Just because it's taking a long time doesn't mean God ran out of options. Your mind is saying, *It's over.* Your emotions are saying, *No way.* The circumstances look impossible. That doesn't mean God won't do what He said.

> *Just because you don't see anything happening doesn't mean God is not working.*

God is faithful to His word. All of His promises are "Yes" and "Amen." That means if you will do your part and believe even though it looks impossible, and not let your mind, your emotions, or other people talk you out of it, then God promises in due season and at the right time He will bring it to pass. It may not happen the way you expect it or on your timetable, but God is a faithful God. It will happen.

He will not let you down. That's what He said in Hebrews 13: "I will not in any way fail you or leave you without support. Therefore we can say with confidence, 'The Lord is my Helper. I will not be afraid. What can man do to me?'"

You need to let that sink down on the inside: "I will not fail you." God is saying, "Everything will work out. I'm in complete control. I know what the medical report says. I know what the financial situation looks like. I see the people who are coming against you. I know how big your dreams are. And hear me clearly; I will not fail you. I will not let you down. I will not let that problem overtake you. I will cause you to be the overcomer."

God is saying if we will keep our trust in Him, He will always make a way even though it looks like there is no way. He will give you strength for every battle, wisdom for every decision, peace that passes understanding. God will vindicate you for the wrongs that have been done. He will pay you back for unfair situations. He promised He will not only bring your dreams to pass but He will give you even the secret desires of your heart.

Dare to trust Him. Come back to that place of peace. Quit being worried, stressed out, wondering if it will happen. God has you in the palm of His hand. He has never once failed before, and the good news is He is not about to start now.

DAY THREE

· ·

I DECLARE I have the grace I
need for today. I am full of power,
strength, and determination.
Nothing I face will be too much for
me. I will overcome every obstacle,
outlast every challenge, and come
through every difficulty better
off than I was before. This is my
declaration.

· ·

When the people of Israel were in the wilderness headed toward the Promised Land, God gave them manna each morning to eat. It would appear on the ground. But He specifically instructed them to gather up only enough for one day's supply. In fact, if they took more it wouldn't last. It would spoil. In the same way, God doesn't give us grace for a year at a time, a month at a time. No, every twenty-four hours God has a fresh new supply of grace, of favor, of wisdom, of forgiveness.

Every twenty-four hours God has a fresh new supply of grace, of favor, of wisdom, of forgiveness.

How will you make it through the slow season at work? One day at a time.

How will you raise a difficult child? One day at a time.

I heard Corrie ten Boom say something very interesting on this topic. During World War II, she and her Dutch family hid Jews from the Nazis and saved many lives. Eventually she was caught and put in prison. In the concentration camps she saw all kinds of atrocities. She even witnessed the deaths of her own father and sister. Through a series of unusual events Corrie was accidentally released and her life was spared. In spite of seeing all the senseless killings she never really became bitter. She even forgave the man who killed her family members.

Somebody asked her how she could make it through those dark days of seeing such terrible acts of hatred and still be loving and kind and forgiving. She answered that question with a story. She told how when she was a little girl, her father would take her on train rides throughout Europe. He would always purchase the tickets several weeks in advance. But he would never give her the ticket until right before they were boarding. Of course, she was a small girl, and he was concerned she might lose it or leave it at home. But whenever her father saw the headlights of the train pulling into the station he would hand his little daughter the ticket and they would step onboard together.

Corrie said to the person who asked how she could be so forgiving: "The reason you can't fathom how I could forgive the person who killed my family, how I could not be filled with bitterness and hatred, is because just like my father and our train tickets, God doesn't give us the grace we need until we're about to step onboard. But if you were to ever go through something like I went through I can assure you God's grace will be there to help you make it through the dark valleys and still keep your head held high and your heart filled with love."

Maybe right now you can't see how to overcome an obstacle, accomplish your dreams, or forgive someone who hurt you, but understand that when you get there God will hand you the ticket. He purchased it two thousand years ago on a cross at Calvary.

Now when you come to a dark valley, a difficult season, a sickness, don't worry about it. Your Heavenly Father will hand you the ticket. He will give you the grace, the strength, the favor, the forgiveness, to do what you need to do.

DAY FOUR

....

I DECLARE it is not too late to
accomplish everything God has
placed in my heart. I have not missed
my window of opportunity. God has
moments of favor in my future. He
is preparing me right now because
He is about to release a special
grace to help me accomplish that
dream. This is my time. This is my
moment. I receive it today! This
is my declaration.

....

Many times we put off what we know God wants us to do. Maybe down deep God has been dealing with you about forgiving a wrong, getting back in shape, having a better attitude, spending more time with your family. Or maybe it's a dream or goal that you know you should be pursuing, such as starting a business, writing a book, joining the choir, learning a new hobby.

You know God put it on the inside but so often we make excuses that hold us back. Things like, "I'm too busy. I tried and failed. I'm not that talented. They hurt me too badly."

It's easy to talk yourself out of your dreams and goals. Too many people settle for mediocrity. But the good news is God never aborts a dream. We may give up on them. We may quit pursuing new opportunities, quit believing to overcome an obstacle. But God still has every intention of bringing to pass every dream, every promise, He put in your heart.

You may have put off taking the first step for a week, a year, or twenty-five years, but God is saying, "It's not too late to get started." You can still become everything God created you to be. But you must do your part and move off dead center. You're not too old or too young. You haven't missed your window of opportunity. The dream is still alive on the inside.

You can still become everything God created you to be.

Now you should rise up in faith and say, "This is my time. This is my moment. I'm not settling where I am. I've let excuses hold me back long enough. But today, I will take steps of faith to pursue new opportunities, to explore new hobbies, to break bad habits, to get rid of wrong mind-sets. I know it's not too late to accomplish everything God has placed in my heart."

If you have this kind of attitude, the rest of your life can be the best of your life. In the Bible when Paul told Timothy, "Stir up the gift. Fan the flame" (2 Timothy 1:6 (NIV), he was saying, "Timothy, life is flying by. Get busy pursuing your destiny."

Every setback means you're one step closer to seeing the dream come to pass.

You have to stay passionate about what God put in your heart. Don't let one disappointment or even a series of disappointments convince you to give up and settle where you are. I've learned every setback means you're one step closer to seeing the dream come to pass. You have to come to your closed doors before you'll ever get to your open doors. You may have tried and failed a thousand times. But you never know; number one thousand and one may be the door that swings open wide. Get your fire back.

You may have been through disappointments. Things might not be the way you'd hoped they would be. Shake off your disappointment. Create a fresh new vision for your life.

DAY FIVE

I DECLARE I am grateful for who
God is in my life and for what He's
done. I will not take for granted the
people, the opportunities, and the
favor He has blessed me with. I will
look at what is right and not what is
wrong. I will thank Him for what I
have and not complain about what
I don't have. I will see each day
as a gift from God. My heart will
overflow with praise and gratitude
for all of His goodness. This is
my declaration.

Whenever I talk to people who have had life-threatening experiences, whether from an illness, an accident, or some other challenge, without fail they talk about how they have come to appreciate each and every day more than ever before. They don't take a minute for granted. They see every day as a gift from God.

We have to realize that our lives could be gone in a moment. There are no guarantees that we will be here at this time next year. Learn to live each day to the fullest. Don't complain. Don't focus on what's wrong. Be grateful for the opportunity to experience each day.

Things may not be perfect. You may have some aches and pains. You may have some adversity. But in the big scope of things your life could be a whole lot worse. And really, you need to live every day like it could be your last.

You need to live every day like it could be your last.

I heard somebody say, "If you only had an hour to live, whom would you call? What would you say? And what are you waiting for?" Don't take for granted what God has already given you.

You may not realize it but we are living in the good old days. I'm convinced twenty or thirty years from now you will look back and say, "Those were some great times. I remember when Lakewood was over in East Houston. I remember when Joel was just a young man. I remember when his brother, Paul, still had some hair!" *These* are the good old days.

I used to play basketball with a young man, a strong athlete, who began having problems with one of his eyes. He went to the doctor and was told that he had a form of cancer that threatened his vision in the eye.

As you can imagine he was devastated. He could not believe it. Then, he went in for surgery and his doctors found that he didn't have cancer. Instead, they found an unusual fungus, which they were able to remove. His vision was saved. When my friend woke up from the operation and heard the good news he said, "This is the greatest day of my life!"

Think about it. He didn't just win the lottery. He didn't just earn a big promotion. He didn't just buy a new home. He simply learned that he would continue to have the vision he'd always had.

He told me, "Joel, now every morning when I get up I

look around on purpose. I stare at my children. I go outside and I look up at the leaves. I take time to pick up an acorn and I'll just stare at it."

Because he almost lost his vision, seeing has now taken on a whole new meaning. He appreciates it in a much greater way.

DAY SIX

....

I DECLARE a legacy of faith over
my life. I declare that I will store
up blessings for future generations.
My life is marked by excellence and
integrity. Because I'm making right
choices and taking steps of faith,
others will want to follow me. God's
abundance is surrounding my life
today. This is my declaration.

....

When you hear the word *legacy* you probably think of what you will leave behind or how you will be remembered when you are gone. That's one way of thinking, but there is something even more significant. The Scripture talks about how we can store up mercy for our children and future generations.

You can store up blessings and favor by living a life of excellence and integrity that will affect generations to come. I know I am blessed today because I had parents who honored God. I also had grandparents who prayed for me and modeled a life of excellence.

You are where you are because somebody sacrificed. Somebody prayed. Somebody served. And now God is honoring them by releasing His goodness in your life. None of us got to where we are on our own. In 2 Timothy 1:5 (NIV), the Apostle Paul said, "Timothy, the faith I see in you first dwelt in your grandmother, Lois, and then your mother, Eunice, and now I can see it in you."

Paul was saying, "Timothy, what I see in you didn't start with you. It started because you had a praying grandmother. That woman honored God with her life. She stored up mercy that was passed down to your mother, and now I can see it in you. And the good news is it will not stop with you. It will be handed down from generation to generation."

You may not feel like you have a godly heritage if your parents or grandparents didn't give God the time of day. But you may be reaping the rewards of a legacy left a hundred years ago by a great-great-grandfather or other ancestors. They prayed. They helped others. It was their faith, their life of excellence, that planted the seed, and now God is rewarding them by helping you to live a life of victory.

Scripture tells the story of Joshua and the people of Israel who were in the midst of a great battle. Their leader Moses was on a hill holding up a staff of God in the air. As long as Moses had his hands raised, Joshua and the Israelites would win. But when he grew tired and put his hands down the enemy would start prevailing.

Moses realized what was happening. He asked a couple men to help him keep his hands in the air. But what I want you to see is Joshua was down there winning the battle. He did not realize the only reason he was winning was because Moses was on the hill holding up his hands.

Without Moses doing his part Joshua and the people

of Israel would have been defeated. Your challenge is to live in such a way as to cause others to win. With every right decision you make, you are holding up your hands. You're making it easier on those who come after you. Every time

> *Your challenge is to live in such a way as to cause others to win.*

you resist temptation you are winning for your children.

Every time you are kind and respectful, every time you help someone in need, every time you come to church, serve, and give, you are storing up mercy. It may be for your children, for your grandchildren, or even a hundred years from now for somebody in your family line who will experience God's goodness because of the life you've lived.

DAY SEVEN

· ·

I DECLARE that God has a great
plan for my life. He is directing my
steps. And even though I may not
always understand how, I know my
situation is not a surprise to God.
He will work out every detail to my
advantage. In His perfect timing,
everything will turn out right. This
is my declaration.

· ·

The Scripture talks about how all of our days have been written in God's book. He's already recorded every part of your life from the beginning to the end. God knows every disappointment, every loss, and every challenge. The good news is your story ends in victory. Your final chapter concludes with you fulfilling your God-given destiny. Here's the key: When you go through a disappointment, when you go through a loss, don't stop on that page. Keep moving forward. There's

> *When you go through a disappointment . . . don't stop on that page.*

another chapter in front of you, but you have to be willing to walk into it.

Sometimes we focus too long on trying to figure out why something didn't work out the way we wanted, maybe why a marriage didn't last, or why we weren't given a position we worked hard for. You may not understand everything you've been through. But if you'll just keep pressing forward, not letting the bitterness take root, you will come to a chapter in your future that will pull it all together, a chapter that will cause it to make sense.

Our daughter Alexandra loved to put together puzzles when she was a little girl. Every couple of weeks we bought her a new puzzle to work on with her. Sometimes it would take us two or three days. Invariably, we would find a piece of that puzzle that didn't look like it fit anywhere. After trying every option we could think of, placing the piece here and there without finding a fit, I'd usually come to the conclusion that the manufacturer must have messed up. Maybe they'd included an extra piece by mistake or dropped in a piece from a different puzzle.

Every time that happened, though, we'd discover as the puzzle came closer to being finished that there was a perfect place for that "extra" piece. What was the problem earlier? All the other pieces weren't together yet.

The same might be true for you and your life. You may have issues or challenges that you don't understand. You're wondering, "Joel, if God is so good, why did my life turn out like this? Why didn't I get that promotion? It just doesn't seem to make sense."

Yes, that's true on its own, but it's because you have pieces to your puzzle that have not yet come together. If you will stay in faith, before long you will see how every setback, every disappointment, even a loss, was simply another piece of your puzzle. You may also discover that if this issue or challenge had not happened you would not have become connected to the great things God had in your future.

You may not see it yet, but God has the right pieces to make your puzzle fit together. That puzzle may not make sense right now, but don't be discouraged—there's another piece coming that will pull it all together.

DAY EIGHT

I DECLARE God's dream for my life is coming to pass. It will not be stopped by people, disappointments, or adversities. God has solutions to every problem I will ever face already lined up. The right people and the right breaks are in my future. I will fulfill my destiny. This is my declaration.

A college professor took a group of students to China for a field trip. Several days into the journey the professor experienced incredible stomach pain. He was hurting so badly, the professor asked a friend to call an ambulance. He was rushed to a local clinic.

They were way back in a small town with no big hospitals. The medical staffer in charge noticed that the professor's appendix had ruptured. Poison was spreading throughout his body, but there were no surgeons around. There was little that could be done for the professor, his friend was told.

"I can give him some pain medication, maybe some sleeping pills, but my advice is that he should make peace with his family," the clinic staffer told him.

The professor went into convulsions and passed in and out of consciousness.

Back at home in the States, the professor's father, who is a pastor, began to feel an incredible burden for his son during a service at his church. The pastor tried to ignore the feeling but it just wouldn't go away. Finally, he stopped the service and he said to the congregation, "We must pray for my son. Something is wrong."

They dropped to their knees and prayed.

Back in China at the clinic it was two o'clock in the morning when one of that country's most well-known surgeons walked in—the same surgeon who travels with the U.S. president when he visits China. The clinic staff was amazed to see him.

"I'm here to take care of the American," the surgeon said.

The Chinese surgeon saved the life of the professor with an operation.

The next day the surgeon said to the recovering professor: "Who were those two men that you sent into my office yesterday?"

"I didn't send anybody to you," the professor replied. "I don't know anybody here in China. I've just been here for a couple of days."

"That's odd, because two men came in dressed in nice suits. They looked like they were government officials," the surgeon said. "And they said

God knows how to make it all work out. . . . He is in complete control.

you were a very important person and I needed to be here in the middle of the night to operate on you."

God knows how to make it all work out. Even seven thousand miles away God had people praying. That's why you can live life in peace. God is in complete control. He knows the end from the beginning. God knows what you will need a week from now, a month from now, even ten years from now. And the good news is He's already taking care of you.

DAY NINE

....

I DECLARE unexpected blessings
are coming my way. I will move
forward from barely making it to
having more than enough. God will
open up supernatural doors for me.
He will speak to the right people
about me. I will see Ephesians 3:20,
exceedingly, abundantly, above-and-
beyond favor and increase in my life.
This is my declaration.

....

My friend Samuel always dreamed of starting his own business. Year after year he was faithful to his employer and he was always doing good things for somebody; not just encouraging people but fixing things at their homes, or giving them rides to the airport. He has a giving spirit.

A while back another friend asked him to go to dinner. Samuel thought they were just catching up on old times, but this friend brought a proposal to start a new business. This man already owned a very successful company, but he wanted to start something new. Samuel thought that he just wanted to get his advice about it and maybe get some encouragement. But he said, "No, I don't want just that. I want you to be my partner and we will split it fifty-fifty."

My friend Samuel was really thrilled.

"I'd love to do that but I don't have the funds like you do," Samuel said. "I can't put in fifty percent like you can."

"Don't worry about it. I don't need your funds," the businessman said. "That's taken care of. I just want to bless you because you've always been so good to me."

Now Samuel owns fifty percent of a growing business.

His dream has come to pass. What was that? He walked into a moment of favor that God had already lined up for him.

A business dropped in his lap. In the same way, God has amazing things in your future. He has doors that will open wider than you thought possible. He can bring across your path opportunity that's greater than you can imagine. You may think you've reached your limits, or that you will never accomplish your dreams, never pay off your house, and never leave anything for your children. But you don't know what God has already spoken over you. You don't know the incredible things God has coming your way.

> *God has amazing things in your future.*

The Bible talks about how God rewards faithfulness. Matthew 25:21 says that when you are faithful in the little things that God will give you greater things. When you remain faithful, I believe your payday is coming

God rewards those who seek after Him. If you have been faithful, if you have given and if you have served then God says: "Your payday is on its way." He is about to release a moment of favor that He already has in your future. All God has to do is speak to one person, and your whole life can change for the better.

DAY TEN

I DECLARE that God will
accelerate His plan for my life
as I put my trust in Him. I will
accomplish my dreams faster than
I thought possible. It will not take
years to overcome an obstacle, to
get out of debt, or to meet the right
person. God is doing things faster
than before. He will give me victory
sooner than I think. He has blessings
that will thrust me years ahead. This
is my declaration.

In the first public miracle Jesus ever performed, he turned water into wine at a wedding reception. During this big celebration, the hosts ran out of wine. Jesus' mother, Mary, came up and told Him about the problem.

"Mom, why are you telling me that? I can't do anything about it," Jesus said. "My time has not yet come."

I can imagine Mary just smiled and said to the workers, "Do me a favor. Whatever He asks you to do, just do it."

Mary knew what He was capable of doing.

There were six stone water pots nearby. They held about thirty gallons each. Jesus said to the workers, "Fill those pots up with water."

They filled them up.

Then He said, "Now dip out some of the water"—which was now wine—"and take it to the host of the party."

When the host tasted it, he called the groom over and said, "This is amazing. Most people serve the best wine first and then, after people have had a lot to drink and don't know any better, they'll bring out the less expensive wine. But you've done just the opposite. You've saved the best wine for last."

I've read some on how long it takes to make wine. It's a very lengthy process that begins, of course, with the planting of the seeds. Then it takes several years for the vines to grow and produce grapes. Once the grapes develop and mature and are just right, they must be picked and processed to make the wine. In general it can take three to five years before the first wine can be bottled. And that's just average-quality wine. The better-quality wine takes between five and seven years to make. Aging it for quality and increased value can take decades.

The best wine is often thought to be twenty or thirty years old. Yet, in His first public miracle, Jesus produced the finest-quality wine in a split second, just a moment in time for what normally would take decades to do. So, if you've worried that you don't have enough time to accomplish your dreams and goals, you need to remember that—just as Jesus sped up the winemaking process—God can do in a split second what might otherwise take you many years.

> *God can do in a split second what might otherwise take you many years.*

Maybe it should normally take you twenty years to pay your house off. But the good news is God is in the accelerating business. He can give you one good break that will thrust you thirty years down the road. He can turn your water into wine.

Be encouraged; the God we serve knows how to speed up natural laws. He can take you farther more quickly than you could ever imagine.

DAY ELEVEN

....

I DECLARE Ephesians 3:20 over
my life. God will do exceedingly,
abundantly above all that I ask or
think. Because I honor Him, His
blessings will chase me down and
overtake me. I will be in the right
place at the right time. People will
go out of their way to be good to
me. I am surrounded by God's favor.
This is my declaration.

....

Irene, a friend of mine, was working at home, refinishing a piece of furniture with an electric sander to remove the old stain. It was a tool she'd had for some time. It wasn't in that great of shape. As she was working, one of the main parts broke off and it wouldn't work anymore. So she put the sander and the broken part into a Lakewood Church bag that she'd just happened to have at home. She went up to the hardware store.

This gentleman came over to help her. She showed him the broken part and asked if he had it. He looked at her in the strangest way, almost like this glaze came his eyes and he said, "No, we don't have that part. We don't even carry that model." But he reached up on the shelf and got a brand-new, top-of-the-line sander and said, "Here, I want you to have this. It's our gift to you."

Irene had never even met the man, never seen him before. She was totally taken back. She said, "Are you sure you want to give this to me?"

He said, "Yes. I'm positive. Just go up to the counter and give them my number: 5-5-5."

So she went up to the counter almost in disbelief. There were three registers open. They had five or six people in each line. She stood at the back of the line. All of the sudden the lady working the register looked over and said, "Hey, lady. Come up here. I want to check you out right now."

Irene pointed at herself and said, "Do you mean me?"

She said, "Yes, I mean you, the highly favored woman."

Irene was kind of embarrassed. She didn't want to cut ahead of others, but the lady insisted, so she went up there and showed her the sander and said, "This man said he wanted to give this to me."

She said, "Well, I don't know if he can do that. Who was he?"

"I don't know but he said his number was 5-5-5," Irene said.

She said, "Well, he can do whatever he wants. He's the regional manager."

Just as Irene was about to leave she said to the lady, "By the way, why did you call me up in front of all these people?"

The lady said, "I saw your Lakewood Church bag and I watch every Sunday. And I know anybody that goes to Lakewood has to be highly favored."

I believe that those who stay in faith are highly

favored. You need to prepare for an exceeding, abundant, above-and-beyond life; a life where people go out of their way for no reason to be good to you; a life where you get promoted even though you weren't the most qualified; a life where you find yourself in the right place at the right time.

When you walk in God's favor, His blessings will chase you down and over-take you.

When you walk in God's favor, His blessings will chase you down and overtake you.

DAY TWELVE

....

I DECLARE I am special and
extraordinary. I am not average! I
have been custom-made. I am one
of a kind. Of all the things God
created, what He is the most proud
of is me. I am His masterpiece,
his most prized possession. I will
keep my head held high, knowing
I am a child of the most high God,
made in his very image. This is
my declaration.

....

Psychologists say our self-worth is often based upon what we believe the most important people in our lives think of us. For children most likely that would be their parents. For adults, that could still be a parent, a spouse, a friend, or a mentor.

The problem with this philosophy is that people can disappoint us. They can say things or do things that bring heartache and pain. If we're receiving our value only from those who hurt us, we'll likely feel less and less valuable over time. Sooner or later they will say something that cuts like a knife, or they will show by their actions that we're not really that important.

The key to really understanding and maintaining a true sense of value is to let your Heavenly Father be the most important person in your life. Base your sense of value on what He says about you.

Let your Heavenly Father be the most important person in your life.

When you make mistakes some may criticize and

make you feel guilty, like you're all washed up. But God says, "I have mercy for every mistake. Get up and go again. Your future is brighter than your past."

Others may make you feel like you're not talented, you're not attractive, or you don't have anything special to offer. But God says, "You're amazing. You're beautiful. You're one of a kind."

People may disappoint you and reject you, even say things that can wound your spirit. If you're receiving your value and your worth only from them, you'll go through life feeling inferior, insecure, with little self-worth. But if you will learn to receive your value from your Heavenly Father and listen to what He says about you, then you'll feel accepted, approved, redeemed, forgiven, confident, and secure. You will feel extremely valuable and that's exactly the way God wants you to be.

Ephesians 2:10 says, "You are God's masterpiece." Do you realize a masterpiece is not mass-produced? You didn't come off an assembly line. You're not average. You're not ordinary. You've been custom-made. You are one of a kind. God created you in His very own image. He looks past all those other things and He looks right at you and says, "There's my masterpiece. That's my son. That's my daughter. That's what brings the most joy to my heart."

DAY THIRTEEN

I DECLARE that God is bringing about new seasons of growth. I will not get stagnant and hold on to the old. I will be open to change knowing that God has something better in front of me. New doors of opportunity, new relationships, and new levels of favor are in my future. This is my declaration.

Sometimes the very things that we fight against, the very things that we think are trying to pull us down, are actually the hand of God trying to push us into a new season. God will stir us out of comfortable situations and He'll put us in situations that make us stretch—situations that force us to use our faith. We may not like it. It may be uncomfortable. But God loves you too much to just leave you alone.

Just as God can supernaturally open doors, sometimes He may supernaturally close doors. Nothing happens by accident. God is directing each of your steps. That means if a friend does you wrong, if you go through a setback, if you lose a loved one, you can either embrace that change and God will use it to take you higher, or you can resist it and you'll end up becoming stagnant and settling for mediocrity.

Stay open for change. Don't approach change from a negative point of view. All change is not bad. It may be negative on the surface but remember, God would not allow it if He didn't have a purpose for it. He will use it to stretch you and to hopefully push you into a new dimension. You may be in a perfectly fine situation for years, but all of a sudden you will see a stirring taking place.

Don't approach change from a negative point of view.

Maybe you thought you'd be in your job for another twenty years, but for some reason the people who were behind you are not behind you anymore. You don't have the favor you once had there. It seems like every day is an uphill battle. What is that? That's God stirring things up.

It's easy to become negative or bitter: "God, why is this happening? I thought I had Your favor." But a much better approach is to just stay open and know that God is still in control. If you will embrace that change, the winds that you thought would defeat you will actually push you to your divine destiny.

Maybe you are in a relationship, and deep down you know the person is not good for you. You know this individual is keeping you from being your best. But you may think, *If I make a change I will be alone.* You don't want to rock the boat. That's why sometimes God will turn the boat over. God may force you to move forward, not because He's mean, not because He's trying to make your life miserable, but because He has such a great desire to see you reach your full potential.

So at times He may cause a friend to walk away. He'll stir things up and may even allow a friend to do you wrong, because He knows if He doesn't close that door you will never move ahead. Thirty years later that person would still be dragging you down, keeping you from your destiny. God would not have stirred it up if He didn't have something better in store. Don't fight change; embrace it, and you will step into the fullness of what God has in store.

DAY FOURTEEN

I DECLARE that I will use my words to bless people. I will speak favor and victory over my family, friends, and loved ones. I will help call out their seeds of greatness by telling them "I'm proud of you, I love you, you are amazing, you are talented, you are beautiful, you will do great things in life." This is my declaration.

When you speak the blessing over your spouse, over your children, over your students, or anyone in your life, you are not just using nice words. Those words carry God's supernatural power. They release favor, ability, confidence, and God's goodness in extraordinary ways.

We should make it our mission to speak the blessing into as many people as we possibly can. With our words we can release favor into somebody else's life.

I heard about a small girl who had a cleft lip. Her lip was a little bit crooked and it made her smile awkward.

With our words we can release favor into somebody else's life.

When she was in second grade other students would not play with her because she looked different. She grew up with these incredible insecurities. She just shrunk back, stayed to herself, and didn't really have any friends. One day the school was conducting hearing tests. The teacher had each student walk slowly away from her while the teacher whispered very quietly. The students were told to repeat out loud, in front of the whole class, what the teacher was whispering.

For most students the teacher would make general statements like "The sky is blue. There's a cat outside. Today is Tuesday."

The students would repeat each statement to show they could hear properly.

When it came time for the little girl with the cleft lip, she was nervous and afraid, but after she passed the hearing test the teacher smiled and told her, "I wish you were my little girl."

When she heard the teacher's approval and the blessing spoken over her, it did something on the inside. It gave her a new sense of confidence, a greater self-esteem. Not only that, when the other students heard how much the teacher loved this little girl, their attitudes changed. Now they all wanted to be her friend. They made sure to sit by her at lunch. They started inviting her over to their home after school.

What was that? The blessing was spoken not by a parent but by an authority figure, and it released God's favor in her life in a greater way. When she became a young lady, the little girl often spoke of that day as a turning point in her life.

I think about what might have happened if her teacher

had withheld the blessing. What if she had just said something ordinary? Who knows where that young lady would be today?

It's so simple but it can have such a huge impact. That's why you should get in a habit of speaking the blessing every chance you get.

DAY FIFTEEN

I DECLARE that I have a sound mind filled with good thoughts, not thoughts of defeat. By faith, I am well able. I am anointed. I am equipped. I am empowered. My thoughts are guided by God's Word every day. No obstacle can defeat me, because my mind is programmed for victory. This is my declaration.

Many of God's promises are in the past tense. In Ephesians God says, "I have blessed you with every spiritual blessing." He says in Colossians, "I have made you worthy." In Psalms He says, "I have surrounded you with favor as a shield."

All of those are put in past tense like it's already happened. Now you must do your part and come into agreement with God. You may not feel blessed today. A lot of things may be coming against you with your family, with your finances, or with your health.

Your mind may be telling you, *This isn't for me. No way I'm blessed.*

Instead, you must be bold and say, "God, if You say I'm blessed then I believe I'm blessed. My checkbook may not say I'm blessed. The economy doesn't say I'm blessed. The medical report doesn't say I'm blessed. But God, I know You have the ultimate authority. Since You say I'm blessed, my report is I am blessed."

When you get in agreement with God like that, it

allows Him to release the promises that already have your name on them. You can pull it out of the unseen spiritual realm over into the physical, seen realm. That's what the Bible says: "God speaks of nonexistent things as if they already existed."

But too many people go around thinking, *Well, I wish I was blessed. I wish I had favor.* No, you've got to reprogram your thinking. It says in Psalms that God has already crowned you with favor. You may not realize it, but there is a crown on your head right now and it is not a crown of defeat, of lack, of mediocrity. It is a crown of God's favor.

God has already crowned you with favor.

If you are to activate that favor, you must get in agreement with God by declaring, "I do have favor." You cannot drag through the day thinking, *Why do I always get the short end of the stick? Why do I always have these bad breaks?* When those discouraging thoughts come and try to convince you that nothing good is in store, just as an act of faith you need to reach up and adjust your crown of favor. Make sure it's on straight. God has already blessed you. He has already made you more than a conqueror. He has already given you that crown of favor.

How do you tap in to what God has already done?

Very simple: just act like you're blessed, talk like you're blessed, walk like you're blessed, think like you're blessed, smile like you're blessed, dress like you're blessed. Put actions behind your faith, and one day you will see it become a reality.

DAY SIXTEEN

....

I DECLARE that I will live as a healer. I am sensitive to the needs of those around me. I will lift the fallen, restore the broken, and encourage the discouraged. I am full of compassion and kindness. I won't just look for a miracle; I will become someone's miracle by showing God's love and mercy everywhere I go. This is my declaration.

....

Y ou're never more like God than when you help hurting people. One of our assignments in life is to help wipe away the tears. Are you sensitive to the needs of those around you? Your friends? Your neighbors? Your coworkers?

Many times behind the pretty smile, behind the Sunday praise, there is a person who's hurting. She's alone. His life is in turmoil. When someone is struggling, reach out. Be a healer. Be a restorer. Take time to wipe away the tears.

Your job is not to judge. Your job is not to figure out if someone deserves something, or to decide who is right or who is wrong. Your job is to lift the fallen, to restore the broken, and to heal the hurting.

Too often we become focused on our own goals, our own dreams, and how we can get our mir-acle. But I've learned something that is more important: I can become someone's miracle.

I can become someone's miracle.

There is healing in your hands. There's healing in

your voice. You are a container filled with God. Right now you are full of encouragement, full of mercy, full of restoration, full of healing. Everywhere you go you should dispense the goodness of God.

If you get around me you'd better get ready. You will be encouraged. You may have made mistakes but I will tell you: *God's mercy is bigger than any mistake you've made.* You may have wasted years of your life making poor choices, but I will tell you God still has a way to carry you to your final destination.

You may have had an addiction since you were a teenager. But I will let you know that the power of the Most High God can break any addiction and set you free. That's what it means to dispense good. You lift the fallen. You encourage the discouraged. You take time to wipe away the tears.

Jesus told the story of the Good Samaritan who was riding his donkey and he saw a man on the side of the road beaten and left for dead. He put him on his donkey and took him to a place where he could recover. I love the fact that the Good Samaritan walked so the injured man could ride.

Sometimes you may have to trade places with someone who is hurting. You must be willing to be inconvenienced.

You may have to miss dinner in order to wipe away a tear. You may have to skip working out one night in order to encourage a struggling couple. You may have to drive across town and pick up a coworker who is addicted and take him to church with you on Sunday. If you want to live as a healer, you must be willing to change places with those who are hurting.

DAY SEVENTEEN

....

I DECLARE I will put actions
behind my faith. I will not be passive
or indifferent. I will demonstrate
my faith by taking bold steps to
move toward what God has put
in my heart. My faith will not be
hidden; it will be seen. I know when
God sees my faith He will show up
and do amazing things. This is
my declaration.

....

In the Scripture there was a man who was paralyzed. He would lie in bed at home all day long. One day he heard Jesus was in town teaching people. He convinced four of his friends to carry him on his bed over to the house where Jesus was speaking.

When they arrived the place was packed and they couldn't get in. They had gone to great lengths to get there. I'm sure the four men were tired. I'm sure their backs were hurting and their shoulders were sore. They'd traveled all that way to no avail. What a disappointment. What a letdown. They could have easily become discouraged and said, "Too bad. It's not going to happen."

But not the paralyzed man: he was determined. I can see his four friends turn to take him home. He says, "No, no. We're not heading home just yet. I'm not leaving until I get my miracle."

You are closest to your victory when you face the greatest opposition.

This man understood: You are closest to your victory when you face the greatest opposition. A lot of people give up too easily.

"Joel, I tried but they told me no."

"Tried to get my degree but the college was full."

"I tried to buy that new home but they wouldn't give me a loan."

"We tried to go to Lakewood but the parking lot was just too crowded."

You must be more determined than that. You have to have a "never say die" attitude. If you can't get in the door why don't you try the window? If you can't get through the window why not be bold and go through the roof? That's what this man did in the Bible story.

He said to his friends, "I've got an idea. Take me up on the roof. Cut a hole in it and lower me down so I can have a front row seat there in front of Jesus."

Where there is a will there is a way. They lowered this paralyzed man down on his bed, all curled up, and put him right in front of Jesus. The Scripture in Mark 2:5 begins, "When Jesus saw their faith..."

That's my question for you today. Do you have a faith that God can see? Are you doing something out of the ordinary to show God you believe in Him? It's not enough to just pray. It's not enough to just believe. Like this man, you have to do something to demonstrate your faith.

Jesus looked at the man and said, "Rise. Take up your bed and walk." Immediately, the man got up. He picked up his bed. He went home perfectly whole. But it all started when he dared to do something where God could see his faith.

There were other people in the room who did not get well. What was the difference? This man put action behind his faith. God is looking for people who have a faith He can see. Not just a faith He can hear. Not just a faith that believes, but also a faith that is visible. A faith that is demonstrated. It's one thing to pray. It's one thing to believe. But if you really want to get God's attention, put actions behind what you believe in.

DAY EIGHTEEN

....

I DECLARE breakthroughs are coming in my life, sudden bursts of God's goodness. Not a trickle. Not a stream. But a flood of God's power. A flood of healing. A flood of wisdom. A flood of favor. I am a breakthrough person and I choose to live breakthrough minded. I am expecting God to overwhelm me with His goodness and amaze me with His favor. This is my declaration.

....

In the Bible, King David needed a breakthrough when he faced an impossible situation. He and his men were up against a huge army—the Philistines. They were greatly outnumbered. They had little or no chance of winning. David asked God for help, and God gave David the promise that He would go with them and they would defeat that army.

When David and his men went out, that was exactly what happened. God gave them a great victory. David was so overwhelmed by it, he said in 1 Chronicles 14:11, "God has broken through to my enemies like the bursting forth of water." He named the place Baal-Perazim, which means, "the God of the breakthrough." Notice, David likened God's power to the bursting forth of waters. He described it as a flood. He was saying when the God of the breakthrough shows up and releases His power it will be like a flood of His goodness, a flood of His favor, a flood of healing, a flood of new opportunity.

Think about how powerful water is: three or four feet of water can pick up a huge car that weighs thousands of pounds and move it all around. I've seen, on the news, big floods floating whole houses down the river. Nothing can stop the force of that water. Anything in the way is moved out of its path.

You may have difficulties that look extremely large, obstacles that look impassable, and dreams that appear unobtainable. But know this; when the God of the breakthrough releases a flood of His power nothing can stop it. Your sickness may look big but it's nothing for the God of the breakthrough. It doesn't have a chance when God releases a flood of His healing.

> *When the God of the breakthrough releases a flood of His power nothing can stop it.*

Your opponents may look powerful. They may be bigger, stronger, better equipped, and better financed. But they don't have a chance when God opens up the floodgates of His favor. You need to be ready, not for a trickle, not for a stream, not for a river. No, get ready for a flood of God's favor, a tidal wave of God's goodness, a tsunami of His increase.

You may be thinking "trickle" when God has an entire ocean to work with. You're thinking "stream" when God has a tidal wave. You should enlarge your vision. Dare to stretch your faith. God wants to release His favor like a flood. He wants to overwhelm you with His goodness.

DAY NINETEEN

I DECLARE there is an anointing
of ease on my life. God is going
before me making crooked places
straight. His yoke is easy and His
burden is light. I will not continually
struggle. What used to be difficult
will not be difficult anymore. God's
favor and blessing on my life is
lightening the load and taking the
pressure off. This is my declaration.

Jesus said, "My yoke is easy and my burden is light." God wants to make your life easier. He wants to help you when you're driving in traffic, shopping at the grocery store, raising your children, and dealing with that problem at work. Every day you should thank Him for His anointing of ease.

This is what David did. He declared in Psalm 23, "God anoints my head with oil." Oil makes things flow. Whenever there is friction or things are stuck, oil is used to lubricate it and make it more fluid. That is what God is doing with you when He anoints your head with oil. David went on to say, "Because God has anointed me, surely goodness and mercy will follow me wherever I go." That means things will be easier. What you used to struggle with will no longer be a struggle. For no reason people will want to be good to you. You will get breaks that you didn't deserve. You will have good ideas, wisdom, creativity, and you won't know where it came from. That is the oil God put on you. His anointing of ease.

I was once in a difficult situation I didn't know how to resolve. I was in another city far away from home. I really needed some advice. So I called a friend. He said, "Joel, you really need to talk to one of my associates. He's an expert in this field. He'll be able to help you. But he's out of town for two weeks."

Well, I didn't have two weeks. That was like a lifetime to me. He asked me where I was and I told him. He said, "You've got to be kidding. That man just left two or three hours ago and that's exactly where he's heading."

When he gave me the address I found the man I needed would be less than two miles from where I was staying. When I heard that, I knew God was still on the Throne.

Here we were; both of us thousands of miles from home. We could have been anywhere in the world. What were the chances that we'd end up less than five minutes from each other?

What am I saying? God is directing every one of your steps. He has already lined up solutions to your problems. He has lined up the breaks you need. I want you to go out each day knowing there is favor in your future. There is restoration in your future. There is healing in your future. There are good breaks just ahead of you. If you stay in faith you will see favor that will make your life easier.

God is directing every one of your steps.

DAY TWENTY

I DECLARE that I am calm and peaceful. I will not let people or circumstances upset me. I will rise above every difficulty, knowing that God has given me the power to remain calm. I choose to live my life happy, bloom where I am planted, and let God fight my battles. This is my declaration.

A lady told me about one of her husband's relatives who was very opinionated. He was always making these cutting, demeaning remarks about her. This couple hadn't been married that long. Every time they went to family get-togethers, this relative would say something to offend her. She would get all upset and it would ruin the day. She reached the point where she refused to even go to family events. Finally, she told her husband, "You've got to do something about that man. He's your relative."

She was expecting her husband to say, "You're right, honey. He shouldn't talk to you like that. I will set him straight." But the husband did just the opposite. He said, "Honey, I love you but I cannot control him. He has every right to have his opinion. He can say what he wants to, but you have every right to not get offended."

At first she couldn't understand why her husband wouldn't really stick up for her. Time and time again she would become upset. If this relative was in one room she would go to another. If he went outside she would make sure she stayed inside. She was always focused on avoiding this man.

One day she realized she was giving away her power. It was like a light turned on in her mind. She was allowing one person with issues to keep her from becoming who she was meant to be.

> *When you allow what someone says or does to upset you, you're allowing them to control you.*

When you allow what someone says or does to upset you, you're allowing them to control you. When you say, "You make me so mad," what you're really doing is admitting that you're giving away your power. As long as that person knows they can push this button and you'll respond this way, you are giving them exactly what they want.

People have a right to say what they want, to do what they want, as long as it's legal. But we have a right to not get offended. We have a right to overlook it. But when we get upset and go around angry, we change. What's happening is we're putting too much importance on what they think about us. What they say about you does not define who you are. Their opinion of you does not determine your self-worth. Let that bounce off of you like water off of a duck's back. They have every right to have their opinion, and you have every right to ignore it.

DAY TWENTY-ONE

I DECLARE God's supernatural favor over my life. What I could not make happen on my own, God will make happen for me. Supernatural opportunities, healing, restoration, and breakthroughs are coming my way. I am getting stronger, healthier, and wiser. I will discover talent that I didn't know I had and I will accomplish my God-given dream. This is my declaration.

In the Bible, God promised Sarah she would have a child. At first she didn't believe it. She thought she was too old. I love what God said to her in Genesis 18:14: "Sarah, is there anything too hard for the Lord?"

God says that to each one of us. "Is there anything too hard for Me?" Do you think your dreams are too big for God to bring to pass? Do you think your relationship is too far gone for God to restore? Do you think you just have to live with that sickness the rest of your life?

No, get a new vision today. Put on a new attitude. God is saying, "I am all-powerful. I can turn any situation around."

It doesn't matter what it looks like in the natural world. He is a supernatural God.

The Amplified Bible puts it this way, "Is there anything too wonderful for the Lord?"

God says, "If you'll take the limits off Me I'll amaze you with My goodness. I'll not only meet your needs, I'll take it one step further. I'll give you the desires of your heart" (2 Corinthians 9:8–9 NIV). One translation says, "the secret petitions of your heart." These are your hidden dreams, those secret desires, those promises that you haven't told anybody about. It's just between you and God. Know this today; God wants to bring your secret petitions to pass. Will you get a vision for it? Will you put your faith out there?

Sometimes we think, *God has bigger things to deal with than me getting this business off the ground, or taking this trip overseas to see my relatives. I can't bother God with that. That's not important enough.*

No, it's just the opposite. God is the one who puts the dream in your heart. I know as a parent I love to do good things for my children. I love to make their day. I want you to get a revelation of how much your Heavenly Father is longing to be good to you. He wants to amaze you with His goodness.

> *God is the one who puts the dream in your heart. . . . He wants to amaze you with His goodness.*

When you believe, it sets a series of events into motion. God wants to give you the desires of your heart. I believe even right now, because you're in faith, because you're saying, "Lord, I believe," God is arranging things in your favor. He is lining up the right people, the right opportunities. In the coming days you will see supernatural increase, explosive blessings.

DAY TWENTY-TWO

....

I DECLARE I will live
victoriously. I was created in the
image of God. I have the DNA of
a winner. I am wearing a crown of
favor. Royal blood flows through my
veins. I am the head, never the tail,
above never beneath. I will live with
purpose, passion, and praise, knowing
that I was destined to live in victory.
This is my declaration.

....

It says in Romans 5:17, "We are to reign in life as kings." When God looks at us He doesn't see us defeated, barely getting by, or just taking the leftover positions. Not at all. God sees you as a king. He sees you as a queen. You have His royal blood flowing through your veins. You and I are supposed to reign in life.

Do you know what that word *reign* means? It means, "time in power." God said we're to reign how long? In life. That means as long as you're alive that is your time in power. You don't have a two-year term like a mayor, a four-year term like a president. Your term is to reign every single day, to be victorious, to rise to new levels, to accomplish great things.

And on those days where you don't feel like a king, or you don't feel like a queen, just remember to reach down and check your pulse, and as long as you feel something beating you can say, "What do you know? It's still my time to reign." Let that be a reminder to put on a new attitude. And sometimes you have to do this by faith. You may not feel victorious. It may not look like you're blessed. But I like that saying, "You've got to fake it until you make it." By faith you need to walk like a king, talk like a king, think like a king, dress like a king, smile like a king. Don't go by what you see. Go by what you know. There is royalty in your DNA. You have the blood of a winner. You were created to reign in life.

Go by what you know.

Too many people are living below their privileges. It's because their vision has been clouded by past mistakes, disappointments, or how they were raised. They don't feel like royalty. They don't think they could be successful and really accomplish what God has put in their hearts. But I believe today, as I'm speaking faith into you, something is happening on the inside.

New seeds are taking root; strongholds that may have kept you back for years, even right now, are being broken. You need to rise up and say, "That's it. I'm not settling where I am. I know it's still my time of power. Yes, I may have taken a break for a little while but I've got an announcement. I'm coming back. I will start stepping up to who God created me to be."

DAY TWENTY-THREE

I DECLARE I am a people builder. I will look for opportunities to encourage others to bring out the best in them and to help them accomplish their dreams. I will speak words of faith and victory, affirming them, approving them, letting them know they are valued. I will call out their seeds of greatness, helping them to rise higher and become all that God created them to be. This is my declaration.

Do you know how many people have never been told: "You are a winner"? There are most likely people in your life right now—people you work with, people you play ball with, maybe even your own family members—who are starving for your approval. They are craving for you to speak the blessing over their life.

You don't know what it will mean when you affirm them, when you give them your approval, and let them know in no uncertain terms that you are proud of them and you think they will do great things. Everyone needs to be valued. Everyone needs to be appreciated. Every person needs that blessing.

Everyone needs to be valued. Everyone needs to be appreciated. Every person needs that blessing.

Let me ask you today, what kind of seeds are you planting in your child, in your spouse, in that friend, in that nephew? Are you believing in anyone? Are you taking an interest to see how you can make someone's life better? Listen to their dreams. Find out what God has put in their hearts. Let them know you're behind them. Give them your approval.

If you talk with any successful people they'll tell you somebody believed in them. Somebody planted a seed and encouraged them when they were down. Somebody helped them get a good break. Somebody spoke faith when they didn't think they could do it.

Thomas Edison encouraged Henry Ford. Mr. Ford was introduced to him as "the man trying to build a car that runs on gasoline." When Edison heard it, his face brightened up. He hit his fist on the table and said, "You've got it. A car that has its own power plant; that's a brilliant idea."

Up to that point no one had encouraged Mr. Ford. No one thought it was a good idea. He had just about convinced himself to give up, but along came Edison and spoke faith into him. That was a turning point in Henry Ford's life. He said, "I thought I had a good idea but I started to doubt myself. Then came along one of the greatest minds that's ever lived and gave me his complete approval."

That's what can happen with a simple vote of confidence. We don't realize the power we hold. We don't always realize what it means when we tell somebody, "I believe in you. You've got what it takes. I'm behind you one hundred percent." And really, every one of us should be someone else's number one fan. We should be encouraging them, lifting them when they've fallen, celebrating when they succeed, praying when they're struggling, urging them forward. That's what it means to be a people builder.

DAY TWENTY-FOUR

....

I DECLARE I will speak only positive words of faith and victory over myself, my family, and my future. I will not use my words to describe the situation. I will use my words to change my situation. I will call in favor, good breaks, healing, and restoration. I will not talk to God about how big my problems are. I will talk to my problems about how big my God is. This is my declaration.

....

We need to pay attention to the things we say. I've known people who are always talking about how tired and run-down they are. They say it so much it's become a reality. The more you talk about negative things in your life the more you call them in. So if you wake up in the morning and feel tired and lethargic, instead of complaining, you need to declare: "I'm strong. I'm full of energy. God is renewing my strength. I can do what I need to do today."

Sometimes when we've been traveling a lot and been very busy we'll come to church and Victoria will say, "Joel, I am so tired. Look at my eyes. Can you see how red they are?"

I always say, "No, Victoria. You look great. You look just as beautiful as ever."

She knows me too well. "No, I don't," she'll say. "I know you. You just won't say it."

Victoria is right. I won't agree when she says she looks bad. I don't want to speak defeat. I want to speak victory. I often wonder what she would think if I ever said, "Oh yeah, Victoria. You don't look good at all. You look so tired. Are you really wearing that?"

I'd have to find a ride home! So, I stick to talking with hope. The more we talk about being tired the more tired we become. The more we talk about being depressed the more depressed we'll be. The more you talk about being overweight the more out of shape you will become. Switch over into victory.

Don't talk about the way you are. Talk about the way you want to be.

There is a young lady on staff at Lakewood Church. She told our women's group that every morning before she leaves the house she looks in the mirror and says, "Girl, you are looking good today."

I saw her a while back and asked if she was still doing it. She said, "Yeah. In fact this morning, Joel, when I looked in that mirror I said, 'Girl, some days you look good but today you're looking really good.'"

I encourage you to be bold in the same way. Encourage yourself. Don't speak defeat over your life. Be bold and dare to say, "I look great today. I'm made in the image of Almighty God. I am strong and talented. I'm blessed. I am creative. I will have a productive day."

Encourage yourself. Don't speak defeat over your life.

DAY TWENTY-FIVE

I DECLARE I will not just survive;
I will thrive! I will prosper despite
every difficulty that may come
my way. I know every setback is a
setup for a comeback. I will not get
stagnant, give up on my dreams,
or settle where I am. I know one
touch of God's favor can change
everything. I'm ready for a year of
blessings and a year of thriving!
This is my declaration.

Some people lock into a survival mentality instead of a thriving mentality. They watch so many troubling news reports they decide: "It's so bad. How will I ever make it?"

Just like you can be talked into surviving, I want to talk you into thriving. I realize we need to use wisdom with what God has given us. But I don't believe we're supposed to pull back to where we're not pursuing our dreams anymore so that we don't expect increase or favor. I don't think we should just be holding on, or trying to maintain. That is a survival mentality.

Remember this: as God took the five loaves and the two fish and multiplied it to feed thousands of people, He can multiply what you have. He can multiply your time and help you to get more done.

> *God can multiply your time and help you to get more done. He can multiply your wisdom and help you to make better decisions.*

He can multiply your wisdom and help you to make better decisions.

God is in complete control. When times get tough don't hunker down and think, *Oh, it's so bad. If I can just hold on and make it through another year...*

No, dig your heels in and say, "I'm not just surviving. I will thrive. I'll prosper despite this difficulty."

A young lady told me that she had struggled in her marriage for a long time. She had done her best to keep it together, but it just didn't work out. She said, "Joel, well, at least I survived." She was happy to just make it through, but I could tell the wind had been taken out of her sails. She was a beautiful girl, but she had lost her fire. She'd lost the sparkle in her eyes.

I told her what I'm telling you: You made it through but you can't keep that survival mentality. God has new seasons in front of you. He has new doors He wants to open. He wants the next part of your life to be better than the first part.

A survival mentality will keep you from God's best. Shake it off and say, "God, You promised what was meant for my harm You would use to my advantage. I may have been through the fire, through the famine, through the flood, but I know it's my time for favor. It's my time to see more of Your goodness in my life."

Keep your faith out there. I want you to start expecting God to increase you in a greater way. Start expecting this to be your best year so far!

DAY TWENTY-SIX

....

I DECLARE I will choose faith over fear! I will meditate on what is positive and what is good about my situation. I will use my energy not to worry but to believe. Fear has no part in my life. I will not dwell on negative, discouraging thoughts. My mind is set on what God says about me. I know His plan for me is for success, victory, and abundance. This is my declaration.

....

Fear and faith have something in common. They both ask us to believe something will happen that we cannot see.

Fear says, "Believe the negative. That pain in your side? That's the same thing your grandmother died from. It will probably be the end of you."

Faith says, "That sickness is not permanent. It's only temporary."

Fear says, "Business is slow. You're going under."

Faith says, "God is supplying all of your needs."

Fear says, "You've been through too much. You will never be happy."

Faith says, "Your best days are still out in front of you."

Here's the key: What we meditate on is what takes root. If we go around all day thinking about our fears, playing them over and over again in our minds, they become a reality.

That's what Job said: "The thing I feared came upon me" (Job 3:25).

A man told me that when things were great in his

life—he'd become engaged, his business was blessed—he didn't enjoy it. Instead of thanking God, he was afraid it would not last and that it was too good to be true.

I told him, "You are helping your fears come to pass. When negative thoughts come, don't let take root. Just switch over into faith and say, 'Father, You said Your favor will last for a lifetime. You said goodness and mercy will follow me all the days of my life.'"

That's choosing faith instead of fear.

Today we have so many opportunities to worry and live in fear. People are worried about the economy, worried about their health, worried about their children. But God is saying to you: "Don't use your energy to worry. Use your energy to believe."

> *Don't use your energy to worry. Use your energy to believe.*

It takes the same amount of energy to believe as it does to worry. It's just as easy to say, "God is supplying all of my needs" as it is to say, "I'll never make it."

Don't expect the worst. That's using your faith in reverse.

Instead say, "God, my life is in Your hands. I know You're guiding and directing my steps and I'm not expecting defeat. I'm not expecting failure. I'm expecting to have a blessed year. I'm expecting to go over and not under."

DAY TWENTY-SEVEN

....

I DECLARE I am equipped for every good work God has planned for me. I am anointed and empowered by the Creator of the universe. Every bondage, every limitation, is being broken off of me. This is my time to shine. I will rise higher, overcome every obstacle, and experience victory like never before! This is my declaration.

....

God has equipped and empowered you with everything you need. You don't have to struggle and try to make things happen. It's already in you: the strength, the creativity, the ideas. God's already lined up the right people. He's already given you the breaks you need by anointing you with oil, His blessings and grace.

When I was growing up, I'd play football on the beach with a bunch of my friends. Back then I'd put Hawaiian Tropic tanning oil all over my body to keep from getting sunburned, but it turned out to help my game, too. I'm already kind of fast, but with that oil, nobody could tackle me. Big guys twice my size would grab me but I'd slip right out of their hands. I had an advantage. I was all oiled up.

That's the way it is when you walk in your anointing: things that should bring you down won't. Maybe you were laid off from the job. You should feel discouraged, but instead you stay in faith and you end up finding a better job.

Maybe your discouragement is due to a relationship

that came to an end. You should feel bitter, but instead you stay in faith and God opens up another door to a better relationship.

When you face tough times, remind yourself, "I've been anointed for this. I will not be negative. I will not lose my joy. I will stay full of praise. I know God is in control, and I believe He can take what was meant for my harm and turn it around and use it to my advantage."

God can take what was meant for my harm and turn it around and use it to my advantage.

If you do that, then one day you will look back on your life and realize that you made it through difficult times through the anointing God put on you. He gave you strength when you didn't think you could go on. He gave you joy when you should have been discouraged. He opened up a door when you didn't see any way out. Now you can look back and say with me, "Where would I have been if it had not been for the goodness of God in my life?"

DAY TWENTY-EIGHT

I DECLARE that I will ask God for big things in my life. I will pray bold prayers and expect big and believe big. I will ask God to bring to pass those hidden dreams that are deep in my heart. If certain promises don't look like they will happen, I will not be intimidated and give up. I will pray with boldness, expecting God to show Himself strong, knowing that nothing is too difficult for Him. This is my declaration.

A lot of times we think we're not supposed to ask for too much. After all, we don't want to be greedy. We don't want to be selfish. I have people tell me, "Joel, if God wants me to be blessed, He'll bless me. He's God."

But that's not the way it works. God expects us to ask. James 4:2 says, "You have not because you ask not." If you're not asking for God's favor, His blessings, His increase, then you're not releasing your faith.

I know people who do ask, but they pray such small prayers: "God, if You'll just give me a fifty-cent raise." They act like they are inconveniencing God.

"God if you will just help me survive this marriage," they say.

No, dare to ask big.

Jesus put it this way, "According to your faith it will be done unto you." That means if you pray little you will receive little. But if you learn to pray bold prayers, and big

If you learn to pray bold prayers . . . it allows God to do bit things in your life.

prayers, and expect big, and believe big, it allows God to do big things in your life.

You may have a dream deep down on the inside, but you've never asked God for it. It's not wrong to ask. It's not selfish to ask. God expects us to ask.

The Scripture says in Psalm 2:8, "Ask of Me and I will give you the nations." God is saying, "Ask Me for big things. Ask Me for those hidden dreams that I've planted in your heart. Ask Me for those unborn promises that may seem unlikely to happen in the natural."

In your quiet time—when it's just between you and God—dare to ask Him for your deepest hopes, your deepest dreams. It may seem impossible, but just be honest and say, "God, I don't see how this could ever happen, but I have a dream to start my own business. God, I'm asking for You to help." Or, "God, I'd love to go back to college but I don't have the time. I don't have the money. God, I'm asking You to make a way."

Dare to ask God for your greatest dreams, your greatest desires.

DAY TWENTY-NINE

I DECLARE God is working all
things together for my good. He has
a master plan for my life. There may
be things I don't understand right
now but I'm not worried. I know
all the pieces aren't here yet. One
day it will all come together and
everything will make sense. I will
see God's amazing plan taking me
places I never dreamed of. This is
my declaration.

Everyone deals with disappointments and challenges that don't seem to make sense. It's easy to grow discouraged and think, *Why did this happen to me? Why did my loved one not make it? Why did this person treat me wrong? Why did I get laid off?*

I want you to understand that even though life is not always fair, God is fair. And He promises in Romans 8:28 that all things work together for our good.

I believe the key word is *together*. You cannot isolate a challenge in one area of your life and say, "Well, my whole life is ruined." That is just one part of your life. God can see the big picture.

One disappointment is not the end. Your life doesn't stop because of a single setback. The challenge you are facing is simply one piece of your puzzle. There is another piece coming that will connect it all. It will work together for your good.

Some people become bitter before all their pieces come together. God has promised a great plan for you. He has predestined you to live in victory. When events occur that you don't understand—hard times that don't make sense—don't let yourself be stuck there. God has more pieces coming your way.

You may feel like your life is missing something, whether it's in the area of your finances, your career, or your marriage. But all God has to do is add some to the puzzle, and your life will feel whole and complete. Those new parts may be the right people, the right opportunities, or the right breaks at just the right time.

Don't be impatient. It's not over until God says it's over. If you will keep pressing forward, one day you will look back and see how it all played into a master plan that God had designed for our lives. You have to have a deep inner trust, a confidence down in your heart that says, "I know God has a great plan for my life. I know He is directing my steps. And even though I may not understand this, I know it's not a surprise to God. Somehow, someway, He will work it out to my advantage."

> *Don't be impatient. It's not over until God says it's over.*

DAY THIRTY

....

I DECLARE God is going before
me making crooked places straight.
He has already lined up the right
people, the right opportunities and
solutions to problems I haven't
had. No person, no sickness, no
disappointment, can stop His plan.
What he promised will come to pass.
This is my declaration.

....

A friend told me that he was trying to resolve a legal situation a while back but he ran into a government bureaucrat who told him it would take two years for his transaction to go through. My friend asked very kindly and politely, "Is there any way that it could happen sooner?"

The man, who was the official in charge of that office, answered back very gruffly: "I said it would be two years and I meant it will be two years. The system is all backed up. I've got so much work in front of you. It will be a long time before I get to your paperwork."

My friend did not give up.

"Well, that's fine," he said, "but I will pray and believe that somehow God will cause it to happen sooner."

That made the bureaucrat even more aggravated. And he said back sarcastically, "Pray all you want, but I'm in charge and I'm telling you it will take two years."

Six weeks later the same official called my friend and said, "Come on in. Your paperwork is ready."

My friend thought it was a mistake. "Are you sure it's mine?" he asked.

"Yes, I'm sure," the bureaucrat said.

My friend went there as quickly as he could. He said to the official, "Thank you so much. But I thought you said it would take at least two years."

"I did," the bureaucrat said. "But ever since I met you I can't get you off my mind. I wake up in the morning thinking about you. I eat lunch thinking about you. I go to bed thinking about you. And I am so sick and tired of thinking about you. Take your paperwork and go."

It says in Deuteronomy, chapter 9, "Today you are about to face people much stronger and much more powerful." Then comes the promise: "But the Lord your God will cross over ahead of you like a devouring fire to destroy them. He will subdue them so that you can quickly conquer.'"

You may be facing a situation that seems impossible, like the bureaucrat who frustrated my friend. It may not appear that you have a chance. But God will take care of your enemies so you can quickly conquer them.

It's not by our own strength or by our own power. It's because Almighty God, the One who holds our future in

His hands, is going before us, fighting our battles, making crooked places straight, even causing our enemies to want to be good to us.

Almighty God is going before us, fighting our battles.

DAY THIRTY-ONE

· ·

I DECLARE everything that doesn't
line up with God's vision for my
life is subject to change. Sickness,
trouble, lack, mediocrity, are not
permanent. They are only temporary.
I will not be moved by what I see
but by what I know. I am a victor
and never a victim. I will become all
God has created me to be. This is
my declaration.

· ·

In Scripture, Joseph had a big dream in his heart, and when he was a young man, God promised that he would be a great leader and even help rule a nation. But before that dream came to pass Joseph had many adversities.

His brothers were jealous of him. They threw him into a deep pit. They left him there to die. But Joseph understood what it says in 2 Corinthians 4:18: "The things that are seen are temporary." One translation says the things that are seen are "subject to change. But the things that are unseen are eternal."

The things we see with our physical eyes are only temporary, but the things we see through our eyes of faith are eternal. Yet too often we allow temporary things to discourage us and cause us to give up on our dreams.

> Anything that doesn't line up with the vision God placed in your heart should be seen not as permanent but as subject to change.

Anything that doesn't line up with the vision God

placed in your heart should be seen not as permanent but as subject to change. Joseph understood this principle. When he was thrown into the pit, he knew that his fate did not line up with the vision God had painted on the canvas of his heart.

Joseph saw himself as a great leader, so he didn't get discouraged. He knew deep down that the pit was only temporary. It did not line up with what he saw through his eyes of faith. In a little while a caravan came by, and he was rescued and taken to Egypt.

Joseph worked as a slave for years in Egypt. But once again he didn't get discouraged. He just checked the picture and said, "No, this is not who I am. A slave does not match up with the promise God put in me. This too shall pass."

Year after year there were disappointments, setbacks, unfair situations. He just kept checking the painting God placed in his heart. One day the right doors did open up. Joseph was put in charge over all of Egypt. This time he could finally say, "Now this is permanent. This is what I've seen in my imagination all these years."

We all face disappointments, setbacks, unfair situations. At times you may feel like you've been thrown into a pit. But instead of being discouraged and letting that cloud your vision, just look inside yourself. You will see that pit does not match up with the vision God put in your heart. Like Joseph, you can say: "This is not permanent. This is just another stop on the way to my divine destiny!"

CONCLUSION

One final thought I'd like to leave with you is that if you are going to live in victory, you must have mountain-moving faith. We all face mountains in life. It may be a mountain in your marriage because you don't see how you'll stay together. Maybe it's a mountain in your finances, your health, or your dreams.

A lot of times we pray about our mountains: *God, please help me. God, please make my child straighten up. God, please take away this fear.* And yes, it's good to pray. It's good to ask God to help you. But when you face a mountain, it's not enough to just pray. It's not enough to just believe. It's not enough to just think good thoughts. Here's the key: you have to *speak* to your mountains. Jesus said in Mark 11:23 (KJV): "Whoever will say to this mountain, be removed, and does not doubt in his heart, he will have whatever he says."

You may be praying about things you should be speaking to. You don't need to pray about that fear anymore. You need to say, "Fear, I command you to leave. I will not allow you in my life." If you have health problems, instead of begging God to heal you, you need to declare to that sickness, "Sickness, you have no right in my body. I'm a child of the Most High God. You are not welcome here. And I'm not asking you to leave. I'm not saying, 'Pretty please, do me a favor.' No, I'm commanding you to leave my body."

I've learned if you don't talk to your mountains, your mountains will talk to you. All through the day, those negative thoughts will come. They are your mountains talking to you.

You can sit back and believe those lies, or you can rise up and declare: "I'm in control here. I will not allow my mountains to talk to me. Mountain, I'm saying to you, 'Be removed. You will not defeat me.'"

It's not a coincidence that God chose a mountain to represent our problems. Mountains are big. Mountains seem permanent, as if they'll be there forever. But God says if you speak to the mountains, you will discover they are not permanent.

If you've dealt with long-term sickness, depression, or

addiction, it may seem like it's never going to change, but when you speak words of faith, something happens in the unseen realm. Mountains crumble. The forces of darkness are defeated. The enemy trembles.

When you declare not in your authority but in the authority of the Son of the Living God, then all the forces of heaven come to attention. The mighty armies of the unseen Most High God will stand behind you. Let me tell you, no power can stand against our God. No sickness. No addiction. No fear. No legal trouble. When you speak and you do not doubt, the mountain will be removed.

Now, the mountain may not move overnight. It may look just the same month after month. Don't worry about it. In the unseen realm, things are changing in your favor. When Jesus was walking through a town, he saw a fig tree and went to get something to eat, but the tree didn't have any fruit on it. He looked at the tree and said, "You will not produce fruit anymore."

Notice, Jesus talked to a tree. People of faith talk to their obstacles. Jesus walked away and it didn't look like anything had happened. The tree was just as green and healthy as it was before. I'm sure some of His disciples whispered, "It didn't work. Jesus must have lost His touch because He said for it to die but it didn't die." What they didn't realize was underneath the ground, in the root system, the moment Jesus spoke, all the life was cut off to that tree.

When they came back through the town a little later, the disciples stood there in amazement. They saw that tree withered up, totally dead. In the same way, the moment you speak to your mountains, something happens. In the unseen realm, the forces of heaven go to work. God dispatches angels. He fights your battles. He releases favor. He moves the wrong people out of the way, sending healing, sending breakthrough, sending victory.

You may not see what God has done for some time. That mountain may look just as big and permanent and strong as it was before. But if you will stay in faith and just keep speaking to the mountain, declaring it gone, declaring yourself healthy, blessed, and victorious—one day, all of a sudden, you will see that mountain has been removed.

God will supernaturally do for you what you could not do for yourself. This is what happened to my mother. She was diagnosed with terminal cancer in 1981. And she spent twenty-one days in the hospital. She came home. She and my father went to their bedroom and got on their knees. And they not only prayed and asked God to heal her, but they spoke to the cancer and commanded it to leave.

There is a time to pray. But there is a time to speak. You don't pray about your mountains, you speak to your mountains. You declare that they will go. Jesus didn't pray about the fig tree. He didn't say, "Well, I believe it won't produce any fruit." He commanded it to not produce fruit.

You should declare that your mountains move, whether they are sickness, depression, strife, or division in your family. Declare to each mountain, "Be removed," and you will have what you say.

Here's the key: your mountains respond to your voice. I can speak faith over you all day long. Your friends can build you up with the scriptures. You can put on good music that will encourage and inspire. And all that's important. That's all good.

But your mountain will respond only to your voice. When you rise up in faith and declare, "Sickness, addiction, depression, leave my life. In the name of Jesus, you've got to go," the forces of heaven come to attention.

David spoke to his mountain of an enemy. He looked Goliath in the eyes and declared, "You come against me with a sword and a shield, but I come against you in the name of the Lord God of Israel."

He declared to his mountain, "Goliath, this day the Lord will deliver you into my hands. I will defeat you and feed your head to the birds of the air." David was saying, "You may be big, but I know my God is bigger. And when I speak to the mountain, God has promised it will be removed."

You may feel there are too many obstacles between you and your God-given dreams. You are standing exactly where David stood. It's not enough to just pray about it. It's not enough to just believe that you're going to get better. Now more than ever, you need to declare, "Mountain of debt, mountain of addiction, mountain of depression, it may look like it's over, but I'm here to serve you notice. This is not the end. You will not defeat me. You come against me with natural weapons. But I come against you in the name of the Lord God of Israel. And I know when I call on the name of Jesus all the forces of heaven come to attention. So I declare that you are removed. I will live and not die. I am blessed and I cannot be cursed. I'm a victor and not a victim."

Incredible power is released when we speak to our mountains. But too many times, we talk to God about how big our mountains are when we should be talking to our mountains about how big our God is.

The more you talk about the mountain, the weaker it makes you. "Well, Joel," you may say, "this sickness or these legal problems or these marriage troubles aren't getting any better." When you talk like that, all it's doing is making you weaker in faith and energy. Quit talking *about* the mountain and start talking *to* the mountain.

Declare to that cancer, or addiction or money challenges, as David declared to Goliath: "I will defeat you."

We see this principle from the very start of the Scripture. In the book of Genesis, it says that the earth was without form and void. There was darkness everywhere. Isn't it interesting that things didn't change just because God's Presence was there? The world didn't get better just because God thought, *I wish I had a world. I wish it was all in order.*

Nothing happened until God spoke. He declared to the darkness, "Let there be light." Think about the word *let*. It indicates that something was opposing. If I say, "Let go of my hand," it means that you're holding it or you're opposing it. God declared in the middle of the darkness, in the middle of the opposition, *let there be light.*

In your times of difficulty when it's dark and gloomy, you should speak light to the situation. After church one day a man told me that his graphic design business was failing. He'd lost his major clients, and bankruptcy seemed inevitable. He explained in great detail all the setbacks he suffered and how bad it was and how impossible it looked. He was real good at talking about the problem.

I told him what I'm telling you. You should talk *to* the problem. You should declare light in the middle of darkness. I encouraged him all through the day to declare: "I'm blessed. The favor of God is turning this situation around. God's favor is bringing me new clients. Debt and lack cannot stay in my life. I command those mountains to be removed."

I saw him about six months later, and he was beaming with joy. He said, "Joel, I did just what you suggested. I started declaring favor, by speaking to my mountains and calling light in the midst of the darkness."

At his lowest moment when it looked for sure like the business was going under, he received a phone call out of the blue from a company he had never done business with before. They asked him to make a presentation and he made it. They hired him to do their graphics. Now, that one new client brings in more business than all of his other clients did combined. He is on pace to have a banner year.

Here's what I'm saying: I believe he would still be struggling, maybe even have lost his business, if he had not kicked his faith into action and started speaking to his mountains.

Let me ask you: Are there mountains holding you back today? Is there something keeping you from God's best in your career, your relationships, or your health? Your mind may tell you the mountain is permanent and that it will never change. My challenge to you is to speak to your mountains. You've prayed about it long enough. Now it's time to declare, "Mountain, you are removed. You will not defeat me. I speak favor over this situation."

Remember, your mountain will respond to your voice. There's nothing more powerful than you declaring victory over your life. You probably have talked about the mountain long enough. You need to talk to the mountain. Rise up and declare to the sickness, or the strife, or the depression: "Be removed, you are gone."

When you do that you will overcome obstacles. You will overcome obstacles that once looked permanent. You will accomplish dreams you thought were impossible.

Make this final declaration with me:

"I declare I walk in the blessing of almighty God. I am filled with wisdom. I make good choices. I have clear direction.

"I declare I am blessed with creativity, with good ideas, with courage, with strength, with ability.

"I declare I am blessed with good health, a good family, good friends, and a long life.

"I declare I am blessed with promotion, with success, with an obedient heart, and with a positive outlook.

"I declare whatever I put my hands to will prosper and succeed. I will be blessed in the city and blessed in the field. I will be blessed when I go in and when I go out.

"I declare I will lend and not borrow, and I will be above and not beneath.

"I declare right now that every negative word, every curse that has ever been spoken over me, is broken in the name of Jesus.

"I declare the negative things that have been in my family even for generations will no longer have any effect on me.

"I declare that from this day forward I will experience a new sense of freedom, a new happiness, and a new fulfillment.

"I declare I am blessed!"

I believe in the spiritual realm things have been set into motion. Curses have been broken and blessings are on their way. Start expecting good things. Learn to speak these words of blessing over yourself, your children, your finances, your health, and your future on a regular basis.

If you'll use your words to declare victory and not defeat you'll see God do amazing things, and I believe you'll live the abundant, overcoming, faith-filled life that He has in store.